Paul Martinson's NEW ZEALAND Birds

Title Page:

1989, Oil on panel, 71 × 55cm (28 × 21¾")

A DAY AT THE PARK

Modern girl (Sarah), apprehensively feeding bread to a white goose at Centennial Lagoon, Palmerston North
John and Helen Martinson collection

Paul Martinson's NEW ZEALAND Birds

Grantham House
New Zealand

Acknowledgements

I wish to thank Raewyn Empson, Don Merton and Paula Bell of DOC for their thoughtful comments on parts of the text of this book. Special thanks go to Bill Clinton-Baker (Gladstone) and Andra Krumins (Wellington) for reviewing everything.

Thanks are also due to Martin Bell, Robert Wheeldon, Dick Gill, Sue Anderson, Mike Aviss and all other staff of the National Wildlife Centre, Mount Bruce for all their helpful assistance and for giving me study access to many living and frozen store birds kept at the bird sanctuary.

Thanks to the following for their efforts in helping me complete many of the paintings and drawings in this book: Gary and Georgina Campbell (Eketahuna), Malcolm and Leanne Kennard (Auckland), David Shannon (Nireaha), Kevin Drysdale (Eketahuna), Johnson and Colleen Cleland (Palmerston North), Mike and Diane Wyeth (Masterton), Jim Campbell (Masterton), Marilyn Drysdale (Nireaha) and Kate Drysdale (Nireaha) (for posing as the Edwardian girl), Sarah Martinson (Palmerston North) (for posing as the modern girl), Neville Shakespeare and Ray Cleary (Masterton — Pest Destruction Board), Maura McDonough (Boston, USA), Christine and Paul McKay (Mount Bruce), Buela and Philip Rhodes (Palmerston North) and the staff of the Manawatu Museum (Palmerston North) and, of course, Hobo. A special thanks to typist Joy Harvey for her endurance.

First published 1991

GRANTHAM HOUSE PUBLISHING

P.O. Box 17−256
Wellington 5
New Zealand

© Paul Martinson

All rights reserved.
No part of this publication may be reproduced, stored in a retrieval system or transmitted in any form or by any means, electronic, mechanical, photocopying, recording or otherwise, without the prior written permission of the publisher.

ISBN 1 86934 028 0

Edited by Anna Rogers
Typeset by Setrite Typesetters, Hong Kong
Designed by Bookprint Consultants Limited, Wellington
Printed by Kings Time Printing Press of Hong Kong in association with
Bookprint Consultants Limited, Wellington

1989, Pencil, 32.5 × 49.5cm (12¾ × 19½")

UNTITLED

Edwardian girl taunting hen
Electricorp Marketing collection

For Mum and Dad, Joy and Gary

1988, 1990, Oil on panel, 60 × 46cm (23¾ × 18")

WAIRARAPA SHED DOOR
Light Sussex cross hen and rooster foraging in farmyard.

Contents

Introduction	8
The Fantail	10
The White Heron	12
The House Sparrow	14
The Silvereye	16
The Song Thrush	18
The Welcome Sparrow	20
The Bellbird	22
The Black-backed Gull	24
The Red-billed Gull	26
The Pied Stilt	28
The Black Stilt	30
The Banded Dotterel	32
The Rhode Island Red	34
The Mallard	36
The Yellowhammer	38
The New Zealand Shoveler	40
The New Zealand Pigeon	42
The Giant Canada Goose	44
The Blue Duck	46
The Grey Teal	48
The Saddleback	50
The Mute Swan	52
The Starling	54
The Rook	56
The Australian Magpie	58
The Robin	60
The Black Robin	62
The Kiwi	64
The Tui	66
The Kakapo	68
The Weka	70
The Takahe	72
The Kea	74
The Pukeko	76
The Kokako	78
The New Zealand Falcon	80
The Australasian Harrier	84
The Spur-winged Plover	86
The Morepork	88
The Rifleman	90
The Rockhopper Penguin	92
The New Zealand Kingfisher	94
The Australasian Gannet	96
The Little Shag	98
Bibliography	100

Introduction

In the winter of 1989, the rural cottage in the Nireaha district (near Eketahuna) where I was living was virtually taken over by a host of birds living in the area. The cottage, its many windows opened regularly to allow for the escape of turpentine and paint fumes, was investigated quite thoroughly by these birds throughout the year, with little regard for its human occupant.

First came three magpies which perched on top of a large freezer in an enclosed fibrolite porch at the front of the house. They had discovered the great potential of this 'soundshell' and gurgled to all the world that they were in charge — even at six o'clock in the morning! If I left the warmth of my bed to face a cold, wintry morning and scorned this singing trio, the magpies would very casually fly away, only to return minutes later for an encore.

Next came a pied fantail who would perch on top of an open window and flit tentatively into the living room before quickly departing. Then, early in the spring, 30 or more starlings made their annual kamikaze missions down the outer surrounds of the wood-burner chimney, hoping to find nest sites. Though all these starlings perished when they became trapped in the dark chamber at the base of the chimney, many others were successful in finding suitable nest sites nearby; the carport in particular became a veritable starling rookery.

Some mornings in early summer welcome swallows came flying in the open bedroom window and tripped gracefully around the room before leaving through the same exit. Of course the cottage had all its sparrows nesting in the roof, who would occasionally fly in through open doors and attempt to knock themselves out against the inside of a big plate-glass window; not to mention the numerous shining cuckoos, blackbirds, thrushes and kingfishers who unwittingly tried flying into the house through the other side of the same closed window.

I eventually realised that this feathery invasion was just the tip of an avian iceberg. The flowerbeds around the garden were occasionally visited by passing flocks of silvereyes and goldfinches. Further out, in the many open paddocks of the farm, where hundreds of dairy cows grazed sedately on lush, green grass, large flocks of yellowhammers roamed and fed regularly, creating a colourful spectacle.

Noisy spur-winged plovers ritually drove off passing harriers as nearby pied stilts and grey herons competed peaceably for worms and insects stranded in the wetter areas. Fallow paddocks were a grazing ground for large flocks of paradise shelducks and Canada geese, and ploughed paddocks were regularly the subject of intense inspection by hundreds of rooks and black-backed gulls. A single drain trickling its way through the farm was a breeding ground for mallard ducks and a refuge to a family of pukeko; willows and pines were home to chaffinches, greenfinches, grey warblers and eastern rosellas.

All these and more were living successfully in what initially had seemed a barren land, devoid of even remnants of the huge podocarp forest which had dominated the ecology of the area for millions of years. This new, rural landscape, entirely transformed by human habitation, was now home to a new generation of New Zealand birds who had, by various means, adapted to living alongside civilisation and all that it had brought.

Since the land became important for agriculture in the nineteenth century, the vast primordial forests have all but disappeared, along with vast numbers of singing birds; today, remaining native forest stands relatively silent. But perhaps a quiet revolution has been taking place over the past 150 years, as many native bird species have adapted to the deforested landscape, competing for food along with introduced species.

The native pukeko, for example, originally a bird of remote swamp and marshland, has adapted amazingly well to living on farms and in city and suburban areas, such as parks, reserves and golfcourses. Here the birds roam and feed in relative harmony, drawing little attention to themselves despite the fact that they are among New Zealand's most colourful and spirited birds.

Although still found in remaining indigenous forest, native birds such as fantails, bellbirds, tui, grey warblers and silvereyes are now also common in many city and suburban gardens; some species are just as numerous as they have ever been. The New Zealand kingfisher and the small native owl, the morepork, though less evident, are also well represented in these colonised areas and are possibly thriving thanks to the diversity of habitats now available to them.

On farms throughout the country many native birds from families such as gulls, waders and waterfowl which were very restricted in their range are widely dispersed and thriving. Black-backed gulls and pied stilts, for example, have adapted most successfully to living alongside civilisation. These gulls have taken advantage of the variety of foods available at human waste disposal sites, such as rubbish tips, as well as utilising the apparent abundance of invertebrates living in cultivated pasture land. Pied stilts, too, have expanded their range, probably because of a greater availability of food and nesting locations in open country.

Many of New Zealand's unique native species have become extinct since the arrival of humans and other species are still reeling from this cataclysm. But the sight of large forest-dwelling New Zealand pigeons grazing on exposed clover-rich pasture will always offer hope for those bird species which have survived. Despite the fact that New Zealand has been occupied almost entirely by bird fauna for millions of years, people are now undeniably the force driving this country and will no doubt continue to be so. It might be fair to assume, therefore, that if New Zealand is ever to go back to the birds it will almost certainly be because of the birds' successful association with people and all that they have brought with them.

The Fantail

PIWAKAWAKA
Rhipidura fuliginosa

The fantail is undoubtedly one of New Zealand's most popular and best-loved birds. With its splendid fan-like tail and attractively coloured plumage, it is certainly one of the prettiest. But the fantail's popularity is not the result of its physical attributes alone. Active the whole day long, the fantail appears to be a very cheerful individual, always announcing its presence with an almost ceaseless stream of chatter in the form of a pleasant, high-pitched 'cheep'. While in pursuit of insects, it delights the observer with aeronautical manoeuvres so masterful they would make the swallow envious.

But the fantail may have won greatest favour for its apparent fearlessness. So many New Zealand homes are visited frequently by fantails which fly in through windows on warm summer mornings to catch house flies. Perching occasionally on light fittings and curtain rails to survey the situation, the birds seem almost oblivious to the human occupants of the house. Having caught a few flies, they flit out through another window and carry on as usual, only to return again the next morning for a repeat of the whole exercise. Despite some superstitions surrounding this aspect of fantails' behaviour ('It's good luck to have fantails in the house', 'No, I'm sure it's bad luck', 'No, isn't it moreporks that are bad luck?'), such visits can surely bring one's home only good fortune.

Prolific breeders, fantails are capable of producing up to four broods in any one year. Their nests, which are started as early as August, are built at the ends of thin branches of shrubs and small trees growing near bush glades and streams, areas which will supply an abundance of flying insects to feed the growing young. Nests started early in the season are usually finished some weeks later, but as the breeding season advances, subsequent nests can be finished off in only a few days.

This is no mean feat when one considers the beauty and complexity of these structures. Composed of many materials such as mosses, leaves, fern fibres and chips of decayed wood all neatly interwoven, then virtually mummified in a sheath of cobwebs, they are superlative little sculptures which would certainly not be out of place in any art gallery.

The fantails' diet consists solely of insects such as moths and flies which are mainly caught on the wing. Fantails often befriend trampers on bush walks in anticipation of insects being disturbed by booted feet. Darting back and forth across walkways, they may follow people for many hundreds of metres before disappearing as quickly as they appeared. They also appear to stir up flying insects themselves by passing quickly through clumps of growing leaves, opening their large tails, almost as if to thrash the bush, then flying out into the open to observe what has been disturbed.

There are three subspecies of fantail in New Zealand: North Island, South Island and Chatham Island. There are also pied and black colour phases which interbreed but produce only one or the other offspring. Never really an endangered bird, the fantail has a basically happy history. For a bird that likes clearings in bush to catch its food, the arrival of civilisation must have been a blessing. In fact, the fantail is probably more abundant now than it has ever been and as more gardens and parks continue to be created, this lovable little bird will probably be happy for ever more.

1989, Oil on panel, 42 × 30.5cm (16½ × 12")

TWO FOR TEA

Pied fantail observing German wasp

THE FANTAIL 11

The White Heron

KOTUKU
Egretta alba modesta

The white heron, which is found throughout much of the South Pacific and Asia, has long been revered and admired for its attractive plumage and its incredible gracefulness in flight. Even standing over a pool, this slender white bird seems spectacular, always contrasting with the dark greens of its wetland habitat. It maintains a motionless vigil, as though fixed by its own beautiful reflection, wavering only in the blink of an eye when it spears and swallows a passing fish.

Apart from the breeding season, New Zealand's small population of white herons can be found throughout the country searching for food in estuaries, streams and lakes. They feed on a wide variety of small aquatic animals such as insect larvae, frogs, whitebait and eels.

The only breeding colony of white herons in New Zealand is in the swampy kahikatea forest of South Westland. Here the breeding season, signalled by the arrival of birds from around the country, begins in about August and sees complex courtship displays between pairing birds. The nest is a strong platform of twigs and sticks built high in the tops of ferns and trees. Both parents are involved in the rearing of the young. After the breeding season, the herons once again depart for various wetland habitats throughout the country.

White herons were once slaughtered by Europeans for their decorative plumes and their numbers declined dramatically. Today, because they are protected and their breeding grounds have become a wildlife sanctuary, their numbers have recovered to a stage where they are now stable. Although it seems very unlikely that white herons will ever be widespread and successful in the North Island, their protection will at least allow them to remain colonised in one of New Zealand's last great frontiers—the damp, forested West Coast.

1989, Pencil, 29 × 40cm (11½ × 15¾")

FLYING

The House Sparrow

Passer domesticus domesticus

The house sparrow belongs to the weaver-bird family and although its brown plumage may indeed resemble a number of the earthy-coloured finches now found in New Zealand, some of its closest family relatives are brightly coloured individuals found in warm, dry regions of the African continent. Some believe that humans have always had a special relationship with sparrows, which joined the northward spread of people through Africa and into and throughout Europe and Asia. Though this connection has often favoured the sparrow, which benefits immensely from the clearing of land and the erecting of buildings, it is perhaps a mutually satisfactory relationship, with birds and humans alike gaining something from each other's presence.

Mutual benefit was certainly the case when house sparrows were first introduced into New Zealand by the colonial settlers last century. Plagues of insects were devastating newly developed crops and eating people out of house and home until sparrows brought these pests under control. Unfortunately large numbers of the birds themselves later found sustenance in some of the crops and sparrows soon became major pests in their own right. They have settled down since then and though still considered a nuisance for the way they damage some crops and nest in buildings, sparrows continue to hunt for a wide range of insects and spiders which, without some kind of natural control, might easily become unmanageable.

The breeding season begins about September after the male has put considerable effort into constructing a nest at a suitable site. He may choose a site where other sparrows are nesting or one on its own. Buildings such as houses, barns and woolsheds are all very popular, but nests may also be located in holes in banks, dense foliage and even tall trees. The nest itself is a bulky spherical structure with a side entrance. It is loosely woven from grass, hay and straw, then lined with feathers and other soft materials.

Both parents incubate the eggs and rear the young. In the early stages the growing chicks are fed almost exclusively on large numbers of insects and spiders which the adults must find. This is why sparrows can often be seen hovering relentlessly around window ledges and walls or hanging upside-down studying the undersides of leaves throughout the spring and summer months. Sparrows are prolific breeders and will rear three broods each season.

Since their introduction to New Zealand, sparrows have established successfully in large numbers almost anywhere there is human habitation. Large roosting colonies occupy deciduous trees in city and town centres in the winter months, made more noticeable by the white footpaths beneath them. Most impressive, though, perhaps, is the house sparrows' great ability to build up their population after being poisoned and trapped, an ability which will surely help these little weavers to survive many more centuries with civilisation.

1987, Watercolour, 31 × 42.5cm (12¼ × 16¾")

JUVENILE BEHAVIOUR

Juvenile female house sparrow disturbed by passing bumble bee

THE HOUSE SPARROW 15

The Silvereye

TAUHOU
Zosterops lateralis lateralis

Any New Zealander who has ever owned a cat has quite probably had a tiny, velvety green bird, with a distinctive white eye, deposited on their back doorstep. So common is the sight, in fact, that one could almost be forgiven for thinking that Kiwi cats had acquired a real taste for this little bird, though it is probably more likely a result of the very large numbers of inattentive silvereyes to be found throughout the country. So involved are silvereyes in their endless search for food in our winter gardens that even an inquisitive child could seize one.

Silvereyes live in native and exotic forest, scrub, bushy farmland and most suburban and city areas throughout New Zealand. In the winter, especially, they roam about in large groups, investigating garden shrubbery for all manner of edible morsels and they are never too shy to take advantage of bread, a bag of fat or even an apple on a string put out for them by thoughtful humans.

Normally the birds eat a varied diet of caterpillars, spiders, aphids, beetles and fruit. Silvereyes, which belong to a group known as honey-eaters, are also equipped to drink nectar from many flowers, using their special absorbent, fibrous tongues.

The breeding season begins in October when pairs of birds split off from their flocks and build delicate nests, made from a variety of fine materials such as grass, horse hair, fern fibres, moss and lichen. These perfectly formed cup-shaped nests are often suspended between two fine twigs in bushy areas well above ground level. Two broods may be raised in a season, with both parents being involved in rearing the young.

Since their self-introduction from Australia in 1856, silvereyes have adapted successfully to New Zealand. Thriving populations are now found nearly everywhere, and despite their unpopularity with some orchardists and wine-growers who have fruit damaged by the birds, the adorable little silvereyes have won great favour as pest controllers and as welcome members of New Zealand's birdlife.

1989, Pencil, 29 × 41cm (11½ × 16¼")

HAS ANYBODY SEEN KITTY?
Five silvereyes feed on a large red apple, watched by a ginger kitten

The Song Thrush

Turdus philomelos clarkei

Whether it is singing its heart out from the top of a tall tree or pulling a reluctant worm from a lawn, the song thrush has become a familiar and welcome sight throughout New Zealand. Though also found in some tracts of remote forest, the bird seems to have a particular preference for civilisation, where it can investigate lawns, flowerbeds, vegetable gardens and hedgerows for food. The thrush eats a variety of insects, worms, snails, slugs and some small berries. Collections of broken snailshells lying by a post or pile of bricks are always a tell-tale sign of this bird's presence.

At the start of the breeding season, which begins about August, thrushes build well-constructed nests in shrubberies and in hedgerows. The nests are tightly woven, cup-shaped structures of grass, roots and twigs which are then lined with mud and wood chips. The young nestlings are fed by both parents, which may raise as many as three broods each year.

European settlers introduced song thrushes to New Zealand in the middle of last century, and the birds now thrive in most places. The common sight of a young thrush fledgling chirping for its mother as it sits patiently on a lawn (where many cats are known to pass) certainly illustrates how enduring these birds are, and the success of their adaptation to civilisation.

1987, Watercolour, 36 × 27cm (18½ × 15¼")

UNTITLED
Song thrush fledgling on barbed wire fence

The Welcome Swallow

Hirundo tahitica neoxena

The welcome swallow is truly the champion of New Zealand's skies. Zooming around all day in hot pursuit of various flying insects, it remains almost unchallenged. I have even seen the masterful bush falcon look on hopelessly as a pair of swallows hovered around it in mid-flight, as if on some kind of bird world reconnaissance mission. Having seen enough of the falcon, they simply flew off. It seemed very bold, especially since every other bird in the area had darted for cover, fearing the falcon's attack.

Welcome swallows catch various flying insects on the wing and are usually found frequenting waterways such as streams, rivers and lakes where greater volumes of insects may be found. With their long, narrow wings and tail feathers, swallows are superbly designed for high-speed flight and can change direction very quickly when they spot an insect.

The breeding season can begin about August (September in some places) and the cup-shaped nest is built from mud and straw which is fixed onto walls or beams with overhead cover. The undersides of bridges, old barns and sheds, culverts, caves or old water tanks, are all choice nesting locations. Once completed, the nest is usually lined with other materials such as grass and leaves, then, finally, with lots of feathers. Swallows generally attempt to raise two or three broods a year. A pair of swallows nesting in my carport recently raised three young birds and as soon as the young birds had barely begun to feed themselves, the parents had relined the nest with fresh feathers and laid another five eggs.

As a pretty bird, very graceful in the air and eating things we tend to think of as pests, the welcome swallow has endeared itself to many people. Civilisation itself offers this bird no obstacles. Since its self-introduction to this country in the 1950s, the swallow has continued to increase its range and population. It seems very likely that this most welcome little bird will become a more prominent and permanent feature of this country's birdlife.

1988, Pencil, 54 × 42cm (21¼ × 16½")

UNTITLED

Two swallow fledglings resting in window frame of dilapidated Victorian house, Eketahuna

The Bellbird

KORIMAKO
Anthornis melanura

The bellbird is probably best known to most New Zealanders for its song rather than for any outstanding physical features. The male bird produces a variety of magnificent, crystal clear, single-frequency, bell-like tones, which seem to travel long distances in the quiet of early morning. Pairs of birds will often sing together. There are many accounts dating back to early colonial New Zealand, when bellbird numbers were far greater, of bellbirds singing in almost deafening unison.

Bellbirds belong to a family known as honey-eaters, which includes stitchbirds and tui. They draw nectar from flowers of such trees as pohutukawa, rata, kowhai and rewarewa. Very active birds, they show complex social interactions of hierarchy and territorial dominance. Like tui, bellbirds are great mimics and learn to sing by copying other bellbirds around them. When they have been reared in captivity, in the absence of other bellbirds, they will copy just about anything that makes a sound. Ian Bryant, formerly officer in charge at the National Wildlife Centre, Mount Bruce, described one hand-reared bellbird as an 'outstanding mimic', able to copy the sounds of 'black stilts, silvereyes, parakeets, wolf whistles and, believe it or not, passing trucks'.

Nest sites are usually located among tightly woven vines and creepers or fern fronds anywhere from ground level to near the top of the bush or forest canopy. Nesting may begin as early as September and continue through to about January.

Bellbirds were thought to be in danger of extinction when their numbers declined dramatically in the late 1800s. But, since then, the population has recovered and stabilised. They have moved into, and established themselves successfully in, many gardens, orchards and exotic forests where adequate nectar-bearing plants are available (eucalypts are very popular). The continued planting of many flowering and nectar-bearing trees and shrubs in parks, reserves and public gardens must help significantly to ensure the survival, in populated areas, of this bold and inquisitive little songster.

1987, Watercolour, 47 × 39cm (18½ × 15¼")

UNTITLED
Bellbird feeding among kowhai flowers

The Black-backed Gull

KARORO
Larsus dominicanus

As a farmer ploughs a paddock on a dairy farm in the northern Wairarapa, a lone black-backed gull suddenly appears, as though by magic, rests and waits patiently for the tractor to move on. Then, within an hour of the gull's arrival, a dozen or more black-backs have also appeared from nowhere and begun feeding happily on the abundance of tiny animals and vegetation the plough has exposed from the rich soil.

Black-backed gulls feed on a very wide range of foods and are quick to take advantage of most eating opportunities, nearly everywhere from inland pastoral farms to coastal townships. Insects, frogs, mice, eggs, young birds and various plant species are taken from many inland areas. At rubbish tips the gulls search for discarded food; in coastal areas they roam beaches for all manner of dead and living animal life or dive for fish and shellfish in the ocean.

The breeding season gets under way about October. The nests are built, often in colonies, in many exposed locations such as hillsides, dunes, rocky outcrops and open fields. The nests themselves are constructed mainly of grasses and other available plants and shaped loosely into basin-like structures. The parent birds, very protective of their young, are quick to attack those who intrude into the breeding territory, whether harriers or humans.

The changes brought about by civilisation have been of great benefit to black-backed gulls, which have expanded their range and begun to increase in numbers. The clearing of forest has made much more habitat available to the gulls, which are birds of the open country, and because they are so adaptable in their feeding habits they have been able to take advantage of the many human waste disposal sites that litter the country.

1989, Pencil, 56 × 42cm (22 × 16½")

PORTRAIT OF A BLACK-BACKED GULL ON A NIREAHA DAIRY FARM

THE BLACK-BACKED GULL 25

The Red-billed Gull

TARAPUNGA
Larsus novaehollandiae scopulinus

Red-billed gulls have become one of the most familiar sea birds around the coasts of New Zealand. They are particularly common in many coastal towns and cities where their crimson-coloured beaks and feet make them quite noticeable, as they sit patiently on fence railings, signposts and pavements, watching humans and awaiting opportunities to feed.

Their diet is extremely varied and depends very much on what is available. At sea, the birds catch and eat tiny animals such as fish and crustaceans, whereas on land, in open grass areas, they may eat worms and insects. Around rubbish tips, sewage outlets and in city centres they eat human food scraps. Red-billed gulls will also plunder the nests of other birds, taking eggs and chicks, and they often harass and intimidate many other sea birds, forcing them to surrender their own catch.

They generally breed in colonies, beginning to nest in July. The nests, loosely constructed of grasses and seaweeds, are built at ground level on rocky outcrops and sandy areas in such vicinities as remote beaches, islands and other relatively inaccessible areas. The eggs and young are cared for by both parents.

Red-billed gulls have largely benefited from the arrival of European civilisation by quickly adapting to feed on a wide variety of waste products. When one first hears or sees this distinctive bird, one knows that, not far away, land meets sea.

1989, Oil on panel, 60 × 45cm (23½ × 17¾")

BLUE JANDAL
Red-billed gull, resting just above high-tide mark at Riversdale Beach, Wairarapa

THE RED-BILLED GULL 27

The Pied Stilt

POAKA
Himantopus leucocephalus

This very elegant, almost ornamental bird has become a common sight around New Zealand, particularly by estuaries and river flats. The pied stilt is a wading bird, possessing long legs which enable it to walk through shallow waters, probing and scything the muddy or stony bottom in search of aquatic insects and other invertebrates.

The breeding season begins about July and goes through to February. Often breeding in colonies, pied stilts nest on paddocks, riverbeds, estuaries or just about anywhere close to water. The nests, which are built on or near the ground, can range in size from small to large platform-like structures. The use of locally available materials can make a nest look quite inconspicuous. I was once shown a pair of pied stilts nesting in the remains of a turnip paddock which had been chewed out by dairy cattle. The nest, on a hump by a flooded section of the paddock, was a loose assortment of turnip roots which looked as though it might just as easily have been put there by accident. Yet it was sufficient to help camouflage the eggs and keep them off the damp soil.

Pied stilts defend their nest sites strongly by swooping down on intruders, threatening with a 'yipp-yipp' sound. They may even run off — sometimes pretending to be injured — to distract a predator from their eggs or chicks.

Since the arrival of European civilisation, when much of the land was cleared for farming, pied stilts have thrived and expanded their range. While doing so, they have appropriated much of the habitat once occupied by their relatives, the black stilts, which are less aggressive and more specialised birds. The adaptability of the pied stilt has ensured that this attractive wader will be frequently seen throughout New Zealand.

1989, Pencil, 29 × 39cm (11½ × 15½")

PORTRAIT OF A PIED STILT

THE PIED STILT 29

The Black Stilt

KAKI
Himantopus novaezealandiae

It could be said that New Zealand is a land of 3½ million people, 22 million sheep, about 100 billion sandflies and maybe just 70 black stilts. But whereas the people, the sheep and the sandflies are here to stay, the black stilt faces great peril. Because it is one of this country's most endangered birds, a lot of attention is given to this dark wader but, unfortunately, many of the characteristics which make it very special have also made it vulnerable.

The black stilt tends to be a loner, less able to enjoy collective security than its more gregarious and very successful relative, the pied stilt. The eggs and young of black stilts constantly fall victim to cats, ferrets and rats. As a consequence of this continued predation and the loss of their braided riverbed habitat, the remaining few black stilts are now restricted to the mountain lakes and pools or stony river flats of South Canterbury and North Otago. The diversity of skills black stilts possess for raking a living from these bleak watery landscapes has probably saved them until now.

Black stilts feed on aquatic insect larvae, small fish, worms and snails found in and around the swamps, lakes and streams of their domain. Probing and sifting the ground with their long beaks, they may sometimes feed well into the night. The breeding season begins about September when the birds tend to isolate themselves from other stilts. The nest can be a simple depression lined with grass and twigs placed on a mound of grass, stones or on a riverbank. Black stilts can make valiant attempts to protect their young from intruders, but because the nests are built so close to water (a major highway for many predators), the eggs and young face great danger and are often destroyed and killed.

Cats and rats continue to pose problems for black stilts, but cross-breeding with pied stilts could also see the demise of the species in its pure form. Though black stilts prefer to breed with their own kind, a shortage of mates often causes them to mate with agreeable pied stilts, producing hybrid offspring. So as the pioneering pied stilt continues to expand its range, and affections, places such as the aviaries of the National Wildlife Centre at Mount Bruce near Masterton, which successfully breed black stilts in captivity, may one day be the only places where we can see these birds in their original form.

1989, Oil on panel, 60 × 45cm (23½ × 17¾")

WALKING

The Banded Dotterel

POHOWERA
Charadrius bicinctus

Easily recognised by two distinctive bands across its chest (a black band around the base of the neck and a chestnut-coloured band around the breast), the banded dotterel is widespread and abundant throughout inland and coastal New Zealand.

During the breeding season, which begins about September, dotterels build simple nests from 'scrapes' in the ground. Sometimes loosely lined with dry twigs or grass, the nests are located in open country near water such as coastal sand dunes, estuaries or shingle riverbeds. The single brood raised is protected by the territorial parents, which become extremely aggravated by the presence of intruders and will fake injury to lure predators away from the nest or young chicks.

Banded dotterels feed on a wide variety of tiny animal life living in and around their locality. Crabs, spiders, beetles, ants, worms and caddis fly larvae are some of the foods taken, along with the berries of some plants. During the winter months banded dotterels form into flocks ranging widely in search of food. At the end of the breeding season many banded dotterels migrate to Australia or the northern parts of New Zealand, dispersing throughout New Zealand again just before the next breeding season. A subspecies, appropriately named the Auckland Island banded dotterel, remains on the Auckland Islands.

Banded dotterels have probably benefited from the arrival of civilisation. The clearing of forests, especially in coastal areas, has opened up a lot of land suitable for the dotterels' feeding and nesting requirements, giving these attractive little wading birds an opportunity to expand their range and thrive.

1988, Pencil, 30 × 41cm (11¾ × 16¼")

UNTITLED
Banded dotterel resting on riverbed, North Wairarapa
Robert and Judy Hall collection

The Rhode Island Red

The Rhode Island red, seen occasionally in city and suburban areas but more commonly in rural areas, is a magnificent breed of domestic fowl which seems to satisfy nearly every requirement one could ever ask for: plenty of big brown eggs for breakfast and large meaty bodies for the dinner plate. So appealing are these birds that even the New Zealand bush falcon has been known to deviate from its normal duties of devouring tui and kingfishers to sample these poultry delights. Moreover, with its deep chocolate brown/red colour and the rooster's shiny green-black tail feathers, the Rhode Island red is a good-looking individual to boot and a most tolerant and resilient resident of any homestead.

These desirable qualities are a credit to the birds' American creators William Tripp, who, in the 1890s, first crossed a red Malay cock from the south-east coast of Asia with his scrub hens, and then Isaac C. Wilbour, who continued the cross-breeding with some of Tripp's offspring to produce all-purpose birds with larger bodies and bigger, browner eggs.

Since those early days, the efforts of other top breeders have combined to make the Rhode Island red an international champion. In 1951 a pedigree pullet of the breed laid 325 eggs in 336 days, creating a laying record at the Yorkshire Federation Laying Trials. Although the breed is no longer of any great commercial value, the Rhode Island red has been a key factor in the productivity of today's commercial laying hens.

1988, Oil on panel, 71 × 55cm (28 × 21¾")

SUNBATHING

Three Rhode Island red hens and a rooster sunbathing in front of a derelict colonial cottage near Eketahuna
Mike Aviss collection

The Mallard

Anas platyrhynchos platyrhynchos

Since their introduction in the 1860s mallards have become a common sight on ponds and streams in city and suburban areas throughout New Zealand. The species is made especially noticeable by the distinctive black and iridescent green head of the male bird, which contrasts with the rather drab streaked plumage of the female.

The breeding season begins around September. Nests are constructed from available materials such as grasses which are then shaped into small basin-like structures and may be found in a very wide variety of places—rotting logs, thick vegetation, dense grass areas and sometimes even in holes in trees a considerable height above the ground. As with many ducks, the female incubates the eggs and looks after the ducklings with no assistance from the male.

Mallards are dabbling ducks and as such feed on the variety of insects, seeds and aquatic plants which float on or near the water surface. They will also graze and eat a variety of tiny waterlogged animals and plants in flooded fields.

Although the mallard has been able to occupy niches created by civilisation, it has also, to some extent, competed with the native grey duck, with which it has much in common. The grey duck can still be found thriving in more remote areas, but it will probably always face the threat of losing its identity by crossbreeding with the amorous mallard. Unfortunately, female mallards happily breed with male grey ducks, producing a distinctively strong pattern hybrid offspring which is now a common sight on many municipal duck ponds.

1988, Pencil, 30 × 40cm (11¾ × 15¾")

UNTITLED

Mallard/grey duck hybrid, Masterton
Neil and Jude Wright collection

The Yellowhammer

Emberiza citrinella caliginosa

Yellowhammers are attractive yellow and red-brown birds, much the same size as sparrows, found most commonly on farms, but also within cities and suburban areas of New Zealand. Their diet consists mainly of seeds, fruits and other vegetation but they also eat various insects and spiders.

The breeding season begins in late November. Woven nests of fine grass, hair, tiny twigs and roots are built on, or very close to, ground level in dense vegetation such as blackberry, gorse and tussock. Both parents feed the young birds and when the first brood has been reared to independence, a second brood is usually started.

Introduced to New Zealand in the 1860s, yellowhammers have spread and established successfully throughout most of the country. They are a particularly common sight during the winter months when large flocks can be found eating hay fed out to stock in paddocks or in artificial hay feeders. The birds glean seeds and possibly some insects from this hay and always seem to be in perfect harmony with the sheep and cattle as they mingle and feed.

1989, Oil on panel, 55 × 44.5cm (21¾ × 17½")

CALF FEEDER
Yellowhammer feeding in hay fed to calves on a Nireaha dairy farm, near Eketahuna

The New Zealand Shoveler

KURUWHENGI
Anas rhynchotis variegata

Shovelers are dabbling ducks, which use a filter feeding process to sift out insects, plants and seeds from the water surface. While paddling around in ponds, lakes and rivers in much of the low-lying, open country throughout New Zealand, they draw up water and pass it out through filters at the sides of their specially modified bills.

The breeding season starts in October when the birds build nests of fine grass, lined with down. These are commonly located in dense grass areas, sometimes far from water. As with most ducks, male shovelers tend not to have much to do with rearing the young.

In full breeding plumage, the male shoveler is perhaps the most spectacularly coloured of all New Zealand waterfowl. With a red iris to its eye, a bluish head and back, a chestnut breast, a distinctive green patch on the wing (speculum) and orange feet, it never fails to draw a second glance. Duck shooters notice it too — tens of thousands of shovelers are shot every year. Despite this, the national population remains at a very healthy level, the numbers lost being restored before the next duck shooting season. Duck breeders with sufficiently large ponds are beginning to find that the bird can be raised in captivity with considerable success, so it would seem that the colourful shoveler will continue to be among us for a long time to come.

1989, Pencil, 29 × 41cm (11½ × 16¼")

PREENING
Female New Zealand shoveler
Helen Haldane McKay collection

The New Zealand Pigeon

KERERU
Hemiphaga novaeseelandiae

New Zealand pigeons, which are quite solitary birds, are among the biggest pigeons in the world. Their plumage is a spectacular blend of metallic green, blue, purple and reddish brown. They live and feed in the canopy of much of New Zealand's forest, in patches of bush on pastoral farmland and even in some city centres and suburban areas. Though rarely venturing close to people, the big birds often sit quietly in the treetops, sometimes appearing quite unafraid and almost curious, as people walk beneath them.

In his book, *Birds of the Water, Wood and Waste* (1910), H. Guthrie-Smith recounts the detailed events that brought two wild New Zealand pigeons out of the bush near his Tutira homestead in Hawke's Bay, calmly to perch their clumsy, heavy bodies upon the arms and shoulders of his wife and daughter. These wild birds had freely chosen to join three other very tame, hand-reared individuals in the open garden for a banquet of apple dumpling and bread and were eventually to become so tame — without ever having been held captive — that their wild, skittish behaviour completely disappeared. Although it is difficult to imagine such close encounters occurring today, Guthrie-Smith's experience is certainly a testimony to the trusting and adaptable nature of this very private bird.

The New Zealand pigeons' diet consists of leaves, flowers and fruit from a great variety of plant species. Berries of many podocarp trees such as miro are very popular with the birds, which will gorge themselves to such an extent that they are almost too heavy to fly.

Their breeding season begins about October. The nest, which is usually built high in the bush canopy or in dense foliage well above ground, is a platform-like structure of very loosely arranged twigs. Generally, only one egg is laid and both parents are involved in rearing the solitary young chick.

Two subspecies are found in New Zealand today: the New Zealand pigeon found throughout the country and the Chatham Island pigeon, which is restricted to the Chatham Islands.

The Maori hunted pigeons for food in pre-European times and although the birds appeared to be abundant when the European arrived, their populations may have already begun to decline. Then, with the arrival of the settlers, pigeon numbers suffered drastically through destruction of their habitat and excessive hunting for food and sport. Today they are fully protected and have undergone a recovery which has helped the birds to establish reasonable numbers in many parts of the country. (There is some recent evidence, however, to indicate that some other mainland populations have such a low productivity that they may be very threatened. Continued predation and insufficient food availability may be contributing to this.)

It is now recognised that New Zealand pigeons are essential to forest ecology. They spread the seeds of many forest trees (after fruits have passed through their digestive systems), dispersing the seeds over a wide area and, in doing so, help to maintain the diversity of forest trees upon which so many birds depend.

1989, Oil on panel, 85 × 65 cm (33½ × 25½")

THE LAST BERRY

(A tribute to H. Guthrie-Smith and family)
Edwardian girl feeding coprosma berries to three New Zealand pigeons

THE NEW ZEALAND PIGEON 43

The Giant Canada Goose

Branta canadensis moffitti

A few giant Canada geese, natives of North America, were introduced into New Zealand at the turn of the century. They established themselves in Canterbury and now number in the thousands. As large birds, very fast in flight, they have become keenly sought-after trophies by game bird hunters who travel from all over the country to shoot them. But, just as the 'Canadas' delight hunters by gracing their dinner tables with generous portions, so the hunters, by their actions, ensure that the geese remain in balance with the environment. Were they not controlled effectively, they could easily go through a population explosion which would devastate important farmland in the eastern South Island.

Canada geese eat mainly grasses such as ryegrass and clover and will also take cereals such as wheat and barley. The breeding season begins in September. Nest sites are usually in open country surrounding the headwaters of all major South Island rivers east of the Southern Alps. Mound nests, built from locally available grasses and then lined with feathers, give the parent birds a good all-round view as they incubate their eggs.

1989, Pencil, 29.5 × 39cm (11½ × 15½")

WATCHING

Raana and Jim Campbell collection

The Blue Duck

WHIO
Hymenolaimus malacorhynchos

In mountain streams and rivers of New Zealand, icy blue waters rush headlong over rocky outcrops and fallen forest giants such as rimu and beech. Yet heedless amid all this watery confusion and danger, blue ducks frolic and feed with almost total abandon.

Blue ducks are perfectly adapted to their environment. Coloured in pastel shades of blue, grey and red ochre, they can become almost invisible to the observer. Their feet are relatively large and modified to help drive them forward against the oncoming torrent. They feed on the abundance of aquatic insects, such as caddis fly larvae, which thrive in these oxygen-rich waters. Their bills have rubbery pads at the tip to protect them against damage when the ducks are hunting for food around rock surfaces in the foamy white waters.

Their breeding season starts about August. Nests, which can be built in holes in banks or rotting trees or in dense vegetation close to the water's edge, are made of twigs and grasses loosely put together. The new-born ducklings, which seem very much at home in the turbulent water, are watched over by both parents. The male makes the distinctive high-pitched call, 'whio', which gives the birds their Maori name.

Blue ducks, which are unique to New Zealand, have declined significantly since the beginning of European settlement. The loss of their turbulent river habitat and its marginal strips of vegetation in favour of hydro-electric power stations and the introduction of predators like stoats and rats have caused much damage to the blue duck population. At present there are still a few thousand birds well distributed in the forested, mountainous areas of the North and South Islands. But continued damming and modification of their river habitats could conceivably raise these beautiful mountain ducks' status from threatened to endangered.

1989, Oil on panel, 61.5 × 45cm (24¼ × 17¾")

BLUE DUCK COUNTRY
Blue duck resting by waterfall in Tongariro National Park
Raana and Jim Campbell collection

The Grey Teal

TETE
Anas gibberifrons gracilis

At first glance, this smallish, light grey-brown bird hardly seems to catch the eye, let alone make any noticeable impact on New Zealand's wetlands. But the grey teal (a native of this country and of much of the Australasian region) is relatively well distributed, especially in the North Island. Great travellers, grey teal tend to move about from place to place, no one bird seeming to remain in the same location for too long.

Essentially inland birds, grey teal live on lakes, ponds and swamps where they commonly feed by dabbling the water surface with their bills. This dabbling enables them to filter out seeds and other plant material as well as insects. They will also graze for food on the muddy bottom of their pools as well as from the shores.

The breeding season stretches from June to January. Nest sites were traditionally holes in banks, trees or hollow logs, but with the modifications to the landscape brought about by settlement fewer such sites are now available. It does appear, however, that grey teal have adapted to nesting in ground cover, tussock and sedge. They also take readily to nesting in nest-boxes, if provided. Both parents are involved in looking after the offspring once they have hatched.

Although the grey teal population declined with European colonisation, numbers have since been boosted with the help of the conservation organisation. Ducks Unlimited New Zealand. Making more wetlands available and providing nest-boxes, Ducks Unlimited has helped this little dabbler regain some of its lost ground, making the grey teal somewhat of a success story and perhaps indicating a good future for other similar New Zealand ducks.

1989, Pencil, 30 × 39.5cm (11¾ × 15½")

RESTING

THE GREY TEAL 49

The Saddleback

TIEKE
Philesturnus carunculatus

The saddleback is one of New Zealand's most active and inquisitive birds. At present it lives on offshore islands where it roams beneath the dark forest canopy investigating rotting logs, holes in trees, forest leaf litter and dense vegetation in search of food. Essentially an insectivorous bird, the saddleback eats grubs, cockroaches, moths and wetas, but it also feeds on many berries such as those of coprosmas.

The breeding season begins around September. Nests are built in a variety of places such as the narrow forks of branches, holes in trees and rotting logs and between rock crevices. The nests are loosely constructed of bark fragments, fibres, twigs and grass and lined with some feathers. Saddlebacks lay only two eggs, though there are records of three eggs being laid. Both parents are involved in caring for and raising the chicks.

Two subspecies of saddleback (North Island and South Island) once lived in great numbers throughout New Zealand's forests. The sight of huge flocks of yellowheads, joined by saddlebacks and fantails, moving swiftly and noisily through the South Island bush touched early European settlers with a sense of colour and life which could never be experienced today. Such a friendly and inquisitive bird, always ready to investigate human dwellings and nest in old boots or among farm implements just as starlings might today, was certainly not beyond notice. But sadly, in 1870, when the saddleback became noticeable for its scarcity, it was too late. A host of predators (cats, ferrets, stoats and rats) and perhaps new diseases found the saddleback to be relatively defenceless. Its destruction was nearly complete and by 1890 it was gone from mainland New Zealand, surviving on only two vermin-free offshore islands — Hen Island in the north and around Big South Cape Island in the south.

Today saddlebacks have been introduced to other vermin-free islands around New Zealand and are surviving. Although there are now more saddlebacks, their range is still limited and whereas North Island saddlebacks are considered to be rare, South Island saddlebacks are very much endangered. As it seems very unlikely that they will ever return to the mainland, the future of the saddlebacks will probably always hang in the balance, dependent on human understanding and protection.

1989, Oil on panel, 60 × 45cm (23½ × 17¾")

I LOVE YOU
Two North Island saddlebacks investigating colonial farm building, near Masterton

THE SADDLEBACK 51

The Mute Swan

Cygnus olor

This beautiful white swan was introduced to New Zealand in the 1860s to help adorn parks and gardens. Before 1900 it could be found in such places as the Avon River in Christchurch, but its numbers dwindled there, as in many other places. Competition with the more successful black swan from Australia is often blamed for the mute swan's failure to spread to any great extent.

Mute swans form strong bonds with one another and pair for life. The breeding season begins about September and the birds build massive nests of raupo usually located near the water's edge. Both parents are strongly protective of their eggs and young. Mute swans eat a variety of shoots and leaves of aquatic plant species and probably occasionally fish and frogs.

Found in many public and privately owned lakes and ponds, mute swans are also breeding successfully on Lake Ellesmere and other wetlands in the South Island and some in the North Island. Although they show little sign of greatly expanding their range, these very royal birds will probably always maintain a high profile in the eyes of waterfowl enthusiasts and romantics alike.

1989, Pencil, 47 × 40cm (18½ × 15¾")

UNTITLED
Study of a pair of mute swans

The Starling

Sturnus vulgaris vulgaris

Starlings will nest in a wide variety of confined spaces. Amazingly, their nests have been found in regularly used mailboxes, precariously laid over actively used cropdusting aeroplane engines, in the roofs of houses and the walls of sheds, behind the dashboards of farm tractors, down the vents of chimneys and even behind three emergency toilet rolls which were stacked on top of my own lavatory cistern. Surely, the ultimate act of defiance for some resident starlings in the Mount Bruce area, near Masterton, was to attempt to nest within the confines of a falcon aviary. Needless to say, the starlings were not particularly successful, though the falcons were reported to be doing very well.

The location of the nest site is very important to starlings, and when a mature male has selected a suitable site, he may often have to fight and chase away other starlings to protect it. If he is successful and attracts a mate, serious nesting will begin. Once starlings have set their minds on nesting somewhere, it is often difficult to budge them. The dogged persistence of starlings nesting in a rural mailbox, for example, can be quite extraordinary. Eventually you have to give up! Rather than continuing to clear fresh nesting materials from the box every morning, it can be simpler just to build a nice perch on the mailbox for the convenience of the starlings and ask the rural delivery people to throw the mail out the window as they drive past.

Starlings drink nectar from flowering flax, eat seeds and berries and probe for and catch invertebrates such as insects and spiders. They search for their food in open country, parks, playing fields and gardens nearly everywhere in New Zealand. They can locate grass grubs and worms very effectively by probing the soft ground with their bill, then opening the bill in the ground and peering through the space between the upper and lower mandible to see if they have exposed any evidence of their prey. In cities and suburbs they take advantage of mown grass areas and, in the countryside, like recently grazed paddocks; they will often follow stock around, particularly dairy cattle, which may help to expose the ground surface area for their picking.

In the winter months, starlings like to form roosts, often many thousands of birds strong, in which they spend the nights together, dispersing to a variety of feeding locations the next morning. In some city centres, large flocks of starlings roosting together can cause considerable fouling of footpaths and roadsides, though major 'guano' build-up is not really a problem. One bright suggestion to explain this phenomenon of metropolitan massing is that these roost sites may be strategically chosen by starlings so that their droppings can be recycled back to the suburbs and rural areas by passing vehicles.

Starlings were released in New Zealand during the 1870s and by 1890 were very abundant in many parts of the country. Since then their numbers have been reduced by insecticides, among other things — insecticides kill and poison starlings' food supply — but they seem to have established a balance with the environment. Today they remain a significant feature of this country's resident birdlife. Starlings fill a very important niche made available by the clearing of forest and act as a biological control for many potential pests such as the grass grub. Certainly, in terms of human needs, they can be termed a very important New Zealand bird.

1988, Oil on panel, 71 × 55cm (28 × 21¾")

STARLING FAMILY
Adult starling visiting fledgling on louvre window of old shed, Nireaha, near Eketahuna
Jon Ibbotson collection

THE STARLING 55

The Rook

Corvus frugilegus frugilegus

With its large, dark, glossy beak, 'mouldy' skin-clad face and blue-black sheeny cloak of feathers, the rook has quite a sinister appearance. Like its relatives, the crow and the raven, it would certainly not be out of place in an Edgar Allan Poe novel or an Alfred Hitchcock thriller. And indeed the rook is a bird which should not be underestimated. In some situations its intelligence and cunning make it a fair match for any mere mortal. Just ask anyone who has ever tried to catch or fool this old campaigner; like the chess piece of the same name, the rook always seems to be one move ahead.

Rooks eat a varied and humble diet of insects, worms, spiders, vegetation such as grass and seeds and even rotting flesh. But they also have a liking for walnuts which they actively collect during the autumn and then, like squirrels, take their swag and hide it away for the winter. The nuts are usually buried in an open paddock just below the surface of the ground, then left alone. When retrieved in the winter months, they serve as a very valuable food source.

Rooks will also raid horticultural crops such as maize, barley, peas and wheat when their staple foods are in short supply. This activity, along with damage to pasture and a taste for stock food, gave rooks the doubtful honour of being declared official bird pests. In 1971 controlling their numbers became the responsibility of some Pest Destruction Boards.

Rookeries — rook breeding colonies — are usually built in a single tree or group of large trees with good all-round visibility. Breeding begins around October. There are now rookeries throughout the country, but the rooks' major stronghold remains in the Hawke's Bay region, with other large populations in Canterbury and some in the Wairarapa.

Since their introduction in the early 1860s, to combat insects and remind the colonial settlers of home, rooks have increased in number and spread out relatively slowly. Since they are now kept in check by occasional poisoning, they appear to pose no real threat to New Zealand agriculture in the near future. Moreover, the rooks' call, a harsh 'kaa-kaa', so reminiscent of England, does not always seem out of place in the New Zealand countryside and can even add pleasantly to the daily hubbub of sheep dogs, dog whistles, four-wheel bikes and squabbling magpies.

1989, Pencil, 30 × 41cm (11¾ × 16″)

GOOD FRIENDS

Rook sunbathing upon a scarecrow
Joy and Gary Harvey collection

The Australian Magpie

Gymnorhina tibicen

Magpies living in New Zealand have earned themselves an infamous reputation as very aggressive, territorial birds. Apparently resentful of many intruders near their nesting sites, they have been known to attack and drive off everything from fearsome bush falcons to defenceless children. Cause enough, it would seem, to be very wary of these birds. However, there is also another, very different side to the character of these Australian imports.

Many amusing accounts of magpies raised as pets give telling insights into the birds' nature. One hand-raised young bird, I was informed, could often be found rolling about on the ground with the family cat, or lying on its back playing dead. Sometimes it would swing upside-down on the clothesline, holding on with only one leg from socks or other small articles of clothing. It sounded more like a parrot than a perching bird.

Wild magpies, too, have been known to roll about and play among themselves. Strolling across remote Wairarapa farmland late one afternoon, I came across a group of five magpies, which were quite unaware of my presence, only a few metres away. Four of the birds were watching the fifth member of their group rolling about playfully on its back. At one point this acrobatic individual lay chillingly motionless, feet straight up in the air like some cast sheep, as two other birds ran about shaking their heads and singing. Despite the fact that the inverted magpie remained on its back for nearly 10 minutes, at no point did the others appear to be threatening or intimidating their topsy-turvy friend. Then, when I moved forward, all five birds flew off quite normally, taking with them the secret to their strange game.

The diet of magpies can be quite varied. They eat a variety of insects, spiders and worms, as well as seeds, some plant species, carrion and small animals such as mice and other birds. The breeding season starts about July when magpies build nests, usually located near the tops of tall trees such as pine or macrocarpa. The nests, platform-like structures consisting of many sticks, twigs and mud, can also incorporate cardboard, spoons, sheeps' wool and even various items stolen from clotheslines. The parents defend their nests from intruders, sometimes dive-bombing unwelcome visitors with considerable ferocity.

Two varieties of magpie — black-backed and white-backed — are found in New Zealand, and these can interbreed freely. Since their introduction last century, magpies have spread throughout the country to become a significant and well-established feature of the rural landscape. They were once considered to be the most useful bird ever to be introduced to New Zealand and were protected accordingly. Today, however, they have no protection and must take their chances against the occasional barrage of bullets and verbal abuse. But the magpies appear to be holding their own at this stage, so the melodious, gurgly song of these black and white minstrels will probably continue to be heard over the open green grasslands of New Zealand for a long time to come.

1989, Oil on panel, 60 × 45cm (23½ × 17¾")

THE REAL PANTY THIEVES

Three magpies investigating small articles of clothing on clothesline

The Robin

TOUTOUWAI
Petroica australis

While I was gazing up at the bush canopy in scrub by the Hatepe Stream near Taupo, my attention was suddenly caught by a strange rustling of leaves below. Glancing down, I observed a curious dark, slate-grey bird, all body and spindly legs. Bigger than a sparrow yet smaller than a thrush, it stood there, silent and motionless, only centimetres from my boot. As I moved back slightly, to sit down and get a closer look, the bird suddenly dashed forward to catch and devour about half-a-dozen wriggly things that my scuffing heel had exposed.

This encounter lasted for another half-hour while I continued, deliberately now, to expose the dark, rich soil beneath the dense forest litter. This marvellous, friendly bird was a robin — a North Island robin, to be precise — and I can now appreciate why it has a reputation as one of New Zealand's most enchanting birds. It must endear itself to so many trampers throughout New Zealand with its quiet, inquisitive nature.

Rummaging through the leaf litter of the forest floor, robins feed on invertebrates such as grubs, wetas, worms, caterpillars and spiders. However, they are also known to take their food from trees and shrubs, occasionally going right up into the forest canopy. Robins often befriend people on bush walks for the same reasons as fantails — in anticipation of insects being disturbed from their hiding places. Robins also have a particular preference for investigating campsites in search of food, sometimes venturing into tents and even, on a few rare occasions, perching on people lying still.

Robins can nest in a variety of places — in the forks of branches or in tree trunks, among ferns or in the tangled root structures of old trees. The well-constructed nest, which uses a variety of materials to assist in its camouflage, can easily accommodate up to four chicks. The birds begin laying the first of perhaps three broods as early as August/September. Usually only one brood will be successful as the chicks often fall victim to predators.

Three races of the New Zealand robin exist: North Island, South Island and Stewart Island. The South Island race, with its dark grey back and yellow-white breast feathers, is widely distributed throughout the South Island, whereas the North Island robin is found on offshore islands and the volcanic plateau region, with some populations in the Ruahine Ranges. The Stewart Island bird is similarly isolated in its distribution.

Robins do not like open country, so bush clearance in the North Island saw their numbers reduce dramatically by the turn of the century. However, at present, populations appear stable. Robins do show some ability to adapt to civilisation — birds have been seen in cultivated gardens and exotic forest — and this gives reason to hope that their permanent range will expand, leading to increased numbers of these attractive, friendly birds.

1989, Pencil, 58 × 42cm (22¾ × 16½")

BUSH WALK
North Island robin waiting for tramper's boot to clear leaf litter

The Black Robin

Petroica traversi

The story of the now famous black robin, rescued from certain extinction when only two females of its species remained, is a moving insight into the determination and ingenuity shown by people faced with overwhelming odds. In 1979, when there were only five black robins left in the world, a Wildlife Service team, headed by Don Merton, introduced 'cross-fostering' techniques never before used in New Zealand. They removed eggs from a female named Old Blue (the only effective breeder) and placed them in the nests of Chatham Island warblers.

The Chatham Island warblers became foster parents but were unable to care effectively for the growing black robin chicks so other foster parents had to be found. South Island tomtits were chosen. The tomtits accepted the black robin eggs as their own and could raise black robin chicks to independence. Now Old Blue, having relinquished her parental responsibilities, was free to lay more eggs. These, in turn, were adopted out to willing parents and slowly the black robin population began to recover.

It soon became evident, however, that there was a major problem with this cross-fostering procedure. Some robins raised by tomtits thought they were tomtits themselves! Initially the solution was to return the new black robins (who had become 'imprinted' with tomtit behaviour) to an isolation where they could mix and breed only with their own kind. But in the end, in order to reverse the imprinting, the robin chicks were returned to robin parents before they had fledged (i.e. the tits raised the robin chicks to fledgling age only) and so the young birds grew to independence knowing their true identity.

Black robins feed on a variety of insects and grubs such as tiny wetas, cockroaches and wood borers which they find among leaf litter and attached to rotting logs and vegetation.

They breed between October and December/January, usually raising only one successful brood, if any. One of the causes of the black robins' decline was the fact that they have a low reproductive rate (only two eggs are produced with the entire breeding season required to raise young) and so are unable quickly to regain lost numbers when faced with predation by cats and rats or loss of habitat.

At present, though, black robins are recovering and there are about 100 birds distributed among the Mangere and South-East Islands of the Chatham Island group. With hopes for their repatriation to Pitt Island and perhaps elsewhere in the Chathams, the future of the black robin is certainly brighter now than it has been this century.

1989, Oil on panel, 42 × 30.5cm (16½ × 12")

UNTITLED

Black robin chicks, with parent about to feed wood borer

The Kiwi

Apteryx species

Known to most people, but seen in the wild by few, the kiwi is probably New Zealand's most famous bird. Flightless and nocturnal, it has evolved a perfect adaptation to its forest habitat. On powerful legs, it moves swiftly through the dark, damp forest undergrowth, protected from abrasion and cold by a thick layer of coarse, fibrous feathers. With its powerful sense of smell, using nostrils at the tip of its long beak, and an acute sense of hearing, it can listen and then probe for worms, insects, spiders and other invertebrates moving about in the soil and forest litter. The kiwi also locates and eats some vegetation and fruits that fall to the ground from trees above.

Kiwi breed mainly from July onwards, when a nest made loosely from vegetation is formed in a hollow log, rock crevice or a hole burrowed in the ground. Up to two very large eggs may be laid some days apart, then incubated by the male. The parent birds continue to care for the hatched chicks which, once outside the burrow, are quick to begin feeding themselves.

Three species of kiwi are found in New Zealand today. The brown kiwi, which is the most widely distributed, is found throughout much of the forested area of the North and South Islands and Stewart Island. The little spotted kiwi is found on some offshore islands and the large spotted kiwi is restricted to remote areas of the South Island.

With the arrival of European civilisation, the kiwi suffered greatly when vast tracts of its forest habitat were cleared for farmland. As well suffering predation and destruction by a variety of animals, including cats, dogs and pigs, and over-hunting by people who killed the bird for its meat, the kiwi fell victim to museum showcases and the demand for its feathers. All this caused a great decline in numbers. Today, though, the kiwi is protected, and although little spotted and great spotted kiwi are not as prolific as they once were, the brown kiwi, at least, is holding its own and is very much alive and well in the New Zealand bush.

1989, Pencil, 29.5 × 39cm (11¾ × 15½")

HIDING
Brown kiwi hiding from human intruders

The Tui

Prosthemadera novaeseelandiae

There would not be many New Zealanders who have not, at some stage, noticed the presence of a tui. After all, nearly everything about this bird has been designed to draw attention. Its song and flight displays are a veritable extravaganza, performed, it would seem, to intimidate any passer-by.

Though most of the tui's song is a collection of rather lovely bell-like tones, there is also a great assortment of screechy-scratchy noises which tend to make one feel that not all bird songs were created for human pleasure. Yet perhaps most intimidating of all is the noisy way the tui flies around its domain.

With wing feathers especially modified to make lots of noise in flight, it charges to and fro all day long, harassing other smaller birds which stray into its territory, or venture too close to its food sources.

The tui is a beautifully coloured bird; from a distance it appears quite black, but a closer look will reveal a variety of iridescent green, blue and purple hues. It has a mantle of fine white feathers on the back of its neck and a brilliant white tuft of feathers under its chin.

The tui eats a variety of berries, insects and spiders which it finds by foraging through the bush canopy and around logs and ferns. It will also catch some insects on the wing. A longish, curved bill and a feathery tongue, which acts like a sponge, enable the bird to drink nectar from the flowers of kowhai, flax and pohutukawa. So popular are these flowering plants with the tui, that it is prepared to fly great distances to find them and will often fiercely defend them from other birds, including other tui.

The breeding season extends from September to January. The nest, a loosely woven arrangement of twigs, moss and leaves, is found in dense bushes or in forks of branches of trees or fern fronds. The parent birds are strong defenders of the nest and surrounding area.

Only one species of tui is found throughout New Zealand, with a separate subspecies occurring on the Chatham Islands. The tui has proven to be an adaptable bird, remaining in native forest and establishing itself in exotic forest as well as parks and gardens wherever suitable flowering plants are available. With its rather aggressive approach, always zooming in on the competition with snapping beak and clattery wing feathers, the tui seems intent on remaining a permanent New Zealand resident and perhaps this country's most lovable thug.

1989, Oil on panel, 60 × 45cm (23½ × 17¾")

UNTITLED

Tui perched in flowering kowhai

The Kakapo

Strigops habroptilus

The kakapo, weighing in at over 3 kilograms, is indisputably the world's biggest parrot. Made even more special by its flightlessness and unique nocturnal habits, the species now faces possible extinction; the big bird's kind and gentle nature will always be a vivid memory for those lucky few who have known it, but may remain a mystery to those who, sadly, have not. In a glowing tribute to the kakapo, the naturalist F. W. Hutton described it, in 1923, as one of New Zealand's most remarkable birds. 'Its intelligence,' he said, 'commands respect, and its helplessness sympathy, while its genial nature endears it to all who know it well. It repays kindness with gratitude, and is as affectionate as a dog, and as playful as a kitten.'

The kakapo's diet is made up completely of vegetation and the bird eats everything from roots to fruit from a wide range of forest plants and trees, ferns, lichens, mosses and tussocks.

Breeding between kakapo may occur only every three to four years. Requiring complex and strenuous displays by hopeful males, breeding is made even more difficult and rare by the extreme shortage of females. To attract their mates, male birds excavate 'bowls' or shallow circular depressions in the ground (up to 60 centimetres in diameter) in which they stand and 'boom'. This booming produces low-frequency noises, which (sometimes) attract females.

If a male bird is successful in attracting and then mating with a female, his responsibilities for the breeding season end there, as the female is solely responsible for nesting and for feeding the young. Kakapo nests are known to have been built in rock crevices, under tree roots, in kiwi burrows or as 'scrapes' (shallow depressions) in the ground, and are sometimes loosely lined with wood chips, leaves and grass. Up to five eggs (usually three) may be laid and the hatched chicks are fed on regurgitated vegetation. Since the nest is left unguarded by the lone female, who must go away to gather food, kakapo chicks are always very vulnerable to predators (such as cats and stoats) which may be attracted by the strongly scented tracks, created by the female, leading to the nest.

When European settlers arrived in New Zealand, the kakapo, which before Polynesian inhabitancy had roamed throughout the country, was already in decline. But with the introduction of predators such as cats, rats, stoats and ferrets, the defenceless kakapo vanished from the North Island completely and today is only just surviving on Stewart Island, and on Little Barrier Island and Codfish Island where it has been introduced. With a low reproductive rate and approximately 14 females in existence, the future of the 40 or so remaining kakapo does not look good. Kakapo can be expected to live for perhaps 80 years so there may still be time to relocate the last survivors to other predator-free islands where these splendid moss green parrots can live and breed without restriction.

1989, Pencil, 24.5 × 22.5cm (9½ × 8¾")

UNTITLED

Head study of a kakapo
Dr and Mrs Michael Allan collection

The Weka

Gallirallus australis

The flightless weka is one of New Zealand's most courageous and inquisitive birds. When humans enter weka territory, the birds strut in confidently to inspect and boldly investigate everything from pitched tents to lunch packs. Searching through various belongings (while the owners are present, I might add), they seem to find nearly all human foods to their liking and are always interested in strange new objects, such as shiny cutlery or watches, to the extent that they may very well carry them off.

Lady Barker, in *Station Life in New Zealand*, wrote a most appropriate and revealing description of her encounter with a weka:

> I lay back on a bed of fern, watching the numbers of little birds around us; they boldly picked up our crumbs without a thought of possible danger. Presently I felt a tug at the shawl on which I was lying. I was too lazy and dreamy to turn my head, so the next thing was a sharp dig on my arm, which hurt me dreadfully. I looked round, and there was a weka, bent on thoroughly investigating the intruder into its domain. The bird looked so cool and unconcerned that I had not the heart to follow my first impulse and throw my stick at it; but my forbearance was presently rewarded with a stab on the ankle, which fairly made me jump up with a scream, when my persecutor glided gracefully away among the bushes, leaving me like Lord Ullin, lamenting.

Weka are omnivorous birds, eating fruit and a variety of plant species as well as insects such as wetas or moths and a variety of larger animals such as mice, rats and young birds. Their breeding season begins about July, when nests are built among dense bushes, tussock or rock crevices. The loosely woven nests are constructed mainly of grasses, along with other available materials such as leaves and hair, to form a basin-like structure. Both parents feed and care for the young. Eventually the parents may oust the offspring, forcing them to find new territories. Weka live happily along coastlines, in forests and open country where there is adequate overhead cover. Four subspecies of weka are found in isolated pockets of the New Zealand mainland and on offshore islands.

Since it is a fierce adversary of introduced predators such as rats, stoats and even cats, which have helped to decimate many of New Zealand's other unique flightless birds, it is surprising that the weka is not more widespread. Diseases, possibly spread by domestic poultry, are believed to have wiped out vast numbers of the birds from much of the North Island and some of the South Island around 1920 and their populations have been slow to recover. However, as such a resilient bird, prepared to tolerate humans, the weka will, no doubt, continue to endure civilisation just as civilisation, to some extent, endures the weka.

1989, Oil on panel, 60 × 45cm (23½ × 17¾")

WEKA'S LUNCH
North Island weka investigating a packed lunch
Bluebird Foods collection

The Takahe

Notornis mantelli

The relatively large bulk, ear-rupturing screech and spectacular blue, green and red hues of the flightless takahe belie the fact that the bird, once thought to be extinct, avoided detection in the Murchison Mountains of New Zealand's South Island for decades until 1948, when Dr Geoffrey Orbell found a number of individuals, alive and well, near Lake Te Anau. These days, following extensive scientific study, sophisticated breeding programmes, cameo appearances in television documentaries and numerous 'biographies', the takahe, once shrouded in mystery, has become something of a bird world celebrity and perhaps even a symbol of hope for other lost New Zealand birds, such as the South Island kokako.

The takahe's dense layer of insulating feathers, strong feet and powerful beak equip it well for roaming and feeding in the snowy barren mountains of Fiordland. The diet of the bird in this alpine habitat is derived substantially from tussock, grasses, ferns and insects, though the bird would undoubtedly graze on a far wider variety of plant species were they available.

The breeding season generally begins about October. Nest sites are at ground level and on sheltered locations often surrounded by tussock. The nests themselves are loosely constructed of tussock and grasses to form a basin-like structure. Both parent birds are involved in rearing the fluffy, black chicks and are very protective, attacking and even killing some intruders, such as weasels and rats.

Before the arrival of the Maori in New Zealand, takahe were probably found throughout the country, but by the time European settlers arrived, the bird was restricted to the remote south-west of the South Island. Even their survival in these last frontiers became threatened with the introduction, by Europeans, of deer, which competed for similar foods, and predators such as stoats, which killed young takahe. The birds, now facing a whole new range of problems, disappeared from view. Their rediscovery, which put these colourful, robust birds happily on the road to recovery, will make them familiar to many more generations of New Zealanders.

1988, Pencil, 59 × 42cm (23¼ × 16½")

PORTRAIT OF A TAKAHE IN FIORDLAND

The Kea

Nestor notabilis

The irrepressible kea, New Zealand's answer to Charlie Chaplin, is capable of inflicting mayhem wherever it goes. Humans attempting to live close to these birds in the Southern Alps have been under siege since they arrived. Only mountaineers, tourists and trampers who have little regard for material possessions think nice thoughts about kea.

The stories about their mischievous antics are legion. Just like Chaplin, kea have an uncanny preference for the quality things of life. When visiting unoccupied mountain tramping huts, for example, kea, with the aid of their powerful hooked beaks, seem disposed to disembowel only the very best sleeping bags, often leaving less valuable ones alone. Then, before leaving the hut to continue their rounds, they may investigate all the cutlery, taking it outside for closer inspection. Finally they may rearrange the cooking equipment before emptying a tin of sticky condensed milk over the spare bunk.

But love 'em or hate 'em, you can't escape the fact that these unusual parrots are yet another bird which makes this country unique. Kea are simply unparalleled in the world. No other bird has demonstrated such an all-consuming desire to study the ways of human beings, let alone spend so much time entertaining itself. Kea seem to love skiing down the corrugated iron roofs of huts and other buildings and even down the windscreens of cars, especially those parked in places where humans like to do their own skiing. Should that become a bore, then they can easily play among themselves, happily rolling about chasing and play-fighting one another.

The kea diet includes carrion, fruit and insects. On odd occasions, some birds develop an unfortunate taste for the kidney fat tissue on the backs of live high country sheep. Unable to budge the gorging kea from its back, the sheep can sometimes panic, falling to its death down steep rock slopes while the kea flies off unharmed; or the injured sheep may later die of blood poisoning resulting from the infected wound. Though the kea is a protected native bird, permission can be obtained to shoot offending individuals when necessary. This ensures that such behaviour does not spread to all the kea in the area, which could be disastrous.

The breeding season begins about August/September. The nest, built on the ground using twigs, lichens and leaves, may be located in a sheltered place by rock crevices in forests and clearings. The parents guard the nest site vigilantly against unwelcome intruders and sometimes more than one female is involved in looking after the young.

Once carrying a government bounty over their heads, kea were ruthlessly hunted in the belief that they caused countless sheep deaths. This, however, has turned out to be untrue and the remaining few thousand or so kea, once tens of thousands strong, have the protection necessary to ensure their survival.

1989, Oil on panel, 54.5 × 45cm (24¼ × 17¾")

DAWN RAID
Two kea investigating utensils in mountain hut

THE KEA 75

The Pukeko

Porphyrio porphyrio melanotus

Pukeko are colourful, elegant birds, similar in height to the common or garden hen. Their striking red beaks and legs contrast with their rich velvety blue chests and black back feathers. Outside the breeding season they often travel in family groups which can be seen foraging for food along roadsides and across farmland throughout much of New Zealand.

They are predominantly vegetarian birds, feeding on a variety of seeds, roots, shoots and leaves. Their diet is also supplemented with insects and small animals such as mice and young birds, particularly when they are raising their young.

The breeding season can start as early as September. Nests are located among thick grass, tussock or raupo, built at or near ground level, and often surrounded by or very close to water or boggy ground. Two broods may be raised each season, with both parents being involved in raising the fluffy, black chicks. Pukeko parents are very aggressive defenders of their young, always ready to fight off intruding harriers, rats and cats.

Pukeko adapt very well to being raised with farmyard hens and can make excellent pets if hand-reared from a young age. The strong, determined character of the pukeko never fails to illuminate and inspire the imaginations of small children. The famous New Zealand naturalist, H. Guthrie-Smith, wrote about these birds in 1910: 'Every country place in New Zealand where there are children should rear a family of pukeko. They are delightful pets, and pets, moreover, in absolute freedom who will assert themselves and not be content to tamely starve like the wretched guinea pigs, canaries and rabbits of our youth.'

This strong spirit is probably one of the pukeko's most enduring qualities. Inadvertently, I once directed my dog, Hobo, to catch a rabbit which I had noticed retreating into a lupin bush. Unfortunately the rabbit had scarpered, leaving behind a lone pukeko also taking shelter there. Against his better training (and judgement), Hobo grabbed the poor bird in his jaws, quickly dropping it again when commanded. Rather than flee for its life, the indignant pukeko, only a little the worse for wear, ran after Hobo, pecking him angrily on the backside and causing him to cower and yelp.

But the most significant of the pukeko's qualities has been its ability to adapt quickly to the changes brought to this country by European settlement. Even after the draining of its low-lying swamp and marsh habitat, the pukeko has been able to expand its range to live in and around creeks and ponds scattered across farmland, golfcourses, parks and reserves in most parts of the country. Despite the fact that many duck shooters needlessly kill thousands of these harmless, unpalatable birds every year, the pukeko are, for the moment at least, holding their own and should remain to wander and breed freely over the open lowlands of New Zealand.

1989, Pencil, 57 × 42cm (22½ × 16½")

UNTITLED
Edwardian girl feeding bread to hand-reared pukeko

The Kokako

Callaeas cinerea

The most beautiful bird song I have ever heard would once have heralded many a dark, dank morning in the giant kauri, podocarp and hardwood forests of New Zealand, forests that had stood for millions of years before the onslaught of colonisation. Kokako numbers decreased dramatically in the face of this forest destruction and their sad song seems to echo their plight.

Two subspecies of kokako, North and South Island, once abounded throughout New Zealand and were probably as numerous as bellbirds and tui. Now the North Island kokako is scattered in small numbers — only a few hundred — among the forests of Northland, Rotorua, Taranaki and the volcanic plateau. There have been no confirmed sightings of the South Island kokako for many years, although some recent evidence, which includes the finding of a feather, suggests that they may still exist.

Territorial and known occasionally to fight over boundary lines with their neighbours, kokako are mainly shy by nature and any display of aggression is more bark than bite. They form pair bonds with their mates and are exceedingly affectionate and gentle in these relationships. In their song they always seem to me to be talking to each other in the most intimate way. If you are lucky, kokako may regale you with a collection of melodies which have been compared, by Hutton and Drummond, to 'the notes of a flute exquisitely played upon'.

Kokako belong to the wattlebird family which includes saddlebacks and the extinct huia but, unlike these, they are poor fliers and mainly vegetarian. They move rapidly and efficiently through dense bush by hopping and gliding from one branch to the next, flying only when necessary. Their diet of ferns, mosses, berries, flowers and a wide variety of leaves is supplemented with moths, beetles and scale insects.

They nest in dense thickets of foliage such as bush lawyer and supplejack up to 10 metres above ground level. Although there is much predation of their young from stoats, cats, rats and even native bush falcons, kokako are probably most severely limited in recovering their original numbers by fierce competition for food resources with the introduced opossum. Unfortunately for the kokako, the opossum appears more adept at using these food resources and, for an Australian native, is very successful at rearing its young in New Zealand's climate. It also appears to be expanding its range.

Now rated as one of New Zealand's most endangered birds, the kokako does not seem to face a rosy future. One of the bird's best hopes would probably be the complete annihilation of the opossum, but this is not likely, considering the marsupial's widespread distribution. The kokako may have to compete with opossums and cope with predators if it is to have any long-term successful future on mainland New Zealand. Alternatively, establishing populations of kokako on vermin-free offshore islands may be the only way of ensuring the survival of this very graceful New Zealand songster.

1988, Watercolour, 45 × 35.5cm (17¾ × 14")

PORTRAIT OF A NORTH ISLAND KOKAKO
North Island kokako among wineberry
Lady Diana Isaac collection

The New Zealand Falcon

KAREAREA
Falco novaeseelandiae

The New Zealand falcon, which is unique among falcon species of the world, has justly earned itself a reputation as a fierce hunter. The bird lives a relatively secret and solitary life, but while pursuing its prey it becomes the most deadly, single-minded predator, prepared to chase its quarry through dense thickets of bush, or close to jagged rocky terrain and even into human dwellings, with little regard for the consequences.

Although the falcon can achieve high speeds in its attack approach (up to 200 kph), it still may not be fast enough to catch fleeing tui and pigeons, which can also achieve immense speeds during their dives. The falcon appears to rely on the element of surprise, its superb eyesight and sheer tenacity to catch its prey.

While being chased by a falcon, some birds give truly blood-curdling screams and screeches, not at all typical of normal distress calls, as their perilous journeys through dense cover fail to shake off their determined attacker. Other pursued birds will be driven to perform the most uncharacteristic acts of self-preservation. The shy, secretive New Zealand kingfisher, for example, has been known to take refuge among a group of people walking in an open garden in order to avoid a falcon's attack. Other birds on the run have been known to fly into shops, homes and other buildings through open windows and doors, places normally absolutely off-limits to even the most adventurous feathered individuals.

Despite the falcon's apparent mastery of flight, it continually runs the risk of smashing itself against the many obstacles it encounters in its intense hunting excursions. Its dedication to the pursuit is such that it has been known to wound itself severely or mortally before catching its fleeing victim.

The prey the falcon seeks is extremely varied — from goldfinches and yellowhammers to larger prey such as kaka, grey ducks and farmyard poultry. A falcon will also take lizards and rabbits, as well as large insects such as plague locusts and dragonflies. Despite its great determination when hunting down its prey, the falcon is often unsuccessful and very reluctant to let go of the catch held within the clasp of its large powerful feet. Falcons have been known to hold on doggedly to many a domestic fowl while being pelted with projectiles by the angry owner.

Its occasional taking of domestic birds has probably brought the falcon into greatest disrepute. In the eyes of some, the bird is simply intolerable and it will doubtless continue to be the target of pot-shots taken to defend valuable domestic poultry and waterfowl. Although the New Zealand falcon is fully protected by law, indiscriminate killings will perhaps always feature in the life of this unique species.

Having finally caught its quarry, the falcon may take it back to a regularly used plucking station, such as the top of a cliff or the top of a dead log. Here, all the feathers of small birds are plucked before the flesh is devoured. Small mammals such as rats and rabbits are torn into gobbets or small chunks before being swallowed along with the fur and bones.

The falcon's beak is very sharp and is notable for the irregular or 'toothed' edge visible on the upper half. By holding the food in its feet, the bird can rip and eat through even the toughest of tissues with this beak, crunching bones and cutting tendons with great efficiency. Having consumed enough, the falcon may store the remains of its catch under a bush or rocky outcrop on some hidden bluff, to be retrieved later when hunger returns.

The breeding season begins in September, following courtship displays in which the male often reinforces the pair bonding by

1988, Pencil, 24.5 × 22.5cm (9½ × 8¾")

UNTITLED
Study of a falcon chick
Richard and Karen Gill collection

1988, Pencil, 30 × 40cm (11¾ × 15¾")

UNTITLED
Male eastern falcon, Major, perched and tethered to a block

offering food to his female. The nest sites of falcons, known as eyries, may be established on or near ground level on inaccessible steep cliffs or hillsides which provide both good visibility to the parents and shelter for the young. Shelved areas under overhanging rocks or vegetation are particularly desirable. Up to three eggs are laid directly on the bare soil, blending well into the earth. Both parents are involved in incubating the eggs and rearing the growing chicks.

Intruders to the nest site are forcibly repelled by repeated dive-bombings, in which the falcons may physically strike their unwelcome visitors. People who have entered such nest sites have been violently struck about the head by swooping falcons. Soft protective hats are vital in these situations — they protect human craniums from serious damage and prevent the falcons from breaking their legs when they make contact at great speed.

New Zealand falcons have been used successfully in this country for falconry, both illegally and under the jurisdiction of permit. To date, only one permit has ever been given by the Department of Conservation for keeping and flying falcons.

The falcons Ruth, Major, Liam and Boaz had relatively high public profiles, especially when they were flown experimentally over airport runways in an attempt to scare away birds such as gulls which had become a serious hazard to aircraft. These falcons were also used in public displays, where they were enticed to attack lures to demonstrate various falconry techniques or simply show off their great aerobatic skills. But the most interesting of all this bird's applications would be the chilling spectacle of a fully trained falcon released by the falconer to hunt down a quarry.

The future of the New Zealand falcon is a matter of much discussion in certain quarters. Some sources suggest that the bird is in decline; others suggest that it may be very satisfactorily established throughout New Zealand and even have the potential to expand its range. With the three types of New Zealand falcon (bush falcon, eastern falcon and southern falcon) collectively totalling a possible 3000–4000, well distributed throughout New Zealand, the population seems stable enough for continued success. And the suggestion that some falcons are adapting to changes brought by civilisation (the eastern variety may be feeding almost entirely on introduced birds) is a good indicator that this special and most noble bird will indeed continue to reign as a great hunter.

1988, Watercolour, 38 × 28.5cm (15 × 11¼")

LIAM ROUSING

Study of a male falcon rapidly ruffling its feathers back into position
Maura McDonough collection

1989, Oil on panel, 60 × 45cm (23½ × 17¾")

MAJOR'S BAG

The hunting party: immature male eastern falcon Major, German short-haired pointer and slain Rhode Island red hen

THE NEW ZEALAND FALCON 83

The Australasian Harrier

KAHU
Circus approximans

The harrier has become a common sight along roadsides and over open farmland throughout New Zealand. It is the biggest bird of prey found here and therefore quite distinguishable. Commonly referred to as the 'harrier hawk', the harrier is perhaps the reincarnation of someone who was very wicked in a former life — it is certainly continually chastised by all and sundry simply for being in the vicinity.

Magpies constantly mob and attack harriers for flying over their territory, as do many other birds. There is even one account of an angry mob of sparrows repeatedly dive-bombing a harrier, forcing it to take cover on the ground until they left! Most harriers, however, seem to treat attacks with great indifference and mature birds learn to turn on their backs in flight to fend off attackers with their long, very sharp talons.

The diet of the harrier is quite varied. Opportunists, they will feed on whatever is available. In the winter months they often take advantage of dead animals, such as opossums and hedgehogs, which litter the roads, and in the summer they may feed on other birds, frogs, lizards, insects, mice, rats and rabbits.

The breeding season, which can begin as early as July, starts with elaborate courtship displays between pairing birds. When territories are established, nests are built in low-lying areas near swamps in marshland among ferns, sedges, tussocks and raupo. The nest is often guarded and the parent birds will chase off or attack intruders.

The changes brought by European colonisation have assisted the harrier greatly in expanding its range and increasing its numbers. Because it is essentially a bird of the open country, forest clearance has provided it with more habitat, and the introduction of mammals such as rabbits has meant a wider range of food sources. In addition New Zealand roadsides, littered with dead hedgehogs and opossums, have become a veritable smorgasbord to the harrier, sustaining it during hard times.

1989, Pencil, 56 × 42cm (22 × 16½")

HUNTING STRICTLY PROHIBITED

The Spur-winged Plover

Lobibyx novaehollandiae

The spur-winged plover, so named because it has a protruding, and very sharp, spike or spur at the front of each wing, has had a meteoric rise to success in New Zealand. Following its self-introduction from Australia to southern parts of the South Island, the bird has continued to spread rapidly northwards and can now be found in healthy numbers throughout the country. Spur-winged plovers are colourful, noisy birds which thrive in open country, especially near rivers and streams and other places where the terrain remains wet or damp.

The breeding season begins around June when slightly excavated saucer-like indentations in riverbeds and paddocks are loosely lined with bits of grass and twigs. Generally only one brood is raised by the parent birds, which are very protective of their young. Some intruders will be lured away by an adult bird faking a broken wing. Other intruders such as passing harriers will be swiftly and very noisily repelled with repeated attacks.

Spur-winged plovers eat a variety of worms and insects found around the perimeters of rivers, in neighbouring paddocks and in open pasture country. Co-existing happily with sheep and cattle, and feeding on a variety of tiny animal life on farmlands throughout the country, spur-winged plovers have been welcome immigrants to the wide open spaces of New Zealand and may even have the ability further to expand their range.

1989, Oil on panel, 55 × 44.5cm (21¾ × 17½")

BULLIES
Spur-winged plover and Hereford bull sharing space in an Eketahuna paddock

THE SPUR-WINGED PLOVER 87

The Morepork

RURU
Ninox novaeseelandiae novaeseelandiae

The morepork is New Zealand's best-known owl. Because it is relatively small and very dark in colour, it draws little attention to itself. By day it roosts in dark recesses of the forest or patches of bush, where it sits quietly and harmlessly. During these daytime rest periods, it is sometimes attacked or mobbed by angry groups of birds resentful of its presence. But by night, when all the other birds are roosting, the morepork roams and hunts unchallenged. Like other owls, the morepork has specially modified feathers for quietness in flight. A morepork can easily follow a person with a torch and, despite flying extremely close to catch the insects attracted by the light, give no audible indication of its presence.

The diet of the morepork consists mainly of insects which are caught on the wing or as they move about over rotting logs and tree trunks; wetas are particularly large contributors to the morepork's intake. But the owl will also hunt a wide variety of small birds, mice and rats. Like the New Zealand falcon, the morepork tears its larger prey into gobbets before swallowing the pieces whole.

The breeding season begins in September. The birds create simple nests in hollow tree trunks, burrows in cliffs, among rocks or in very dense vegetation. Both parents may be involved in rearing the young, but the female alone may incubate the eggs. The birds have been known fiercely to defend the nest site, even to the point of physically attacking human intruders.

The morepork has shown itself to be a fairly adaptable bird. Despite the massive changes wrought by European settlement, it is still widely distributed throughout New Zealand, in both native and exotic forests and in city and suburban areas. Although, because of its nocturnal habitats, the bird is seldom seen, it is often heard on quiet nights, uttering the distinctive, eerie call, 'more-pork', which gives it its name.

1989, Pencil, 29 × 41.5cm (11½ × 16¼")

AFTER DARK

Morepork and young opossum sharing space in bush, National Wildlife Centre, Mount Bruce

The Rifleman

TITIPOUNAMU
Acanthisitta chloris

One of the most delightful little birds one could ever hope to encounter in New Zealand bush, the rifleman is tiny in stature, but big in spirit. A pair of the birds will strongly defend their relatively small territory from the intrusion of other riflemen and often appear, from my own observations at least, to protest aggressively at the intrusion of humans. A string of verbal abuse in the form of a high-pitched trill or 'zipp' is delivered from a distance.

Riflemen have very strong legs and feet which they use to cling to branches and tree trunks. They investigate these areas very carefully, starting at a low point and working upwards in search of insects and spiders. In their native subalpine forests they usually nest in holes in trees and rotting logs, but outside their normal domain they have been known to nest in banks, stone walls, clumps of pine needles, nest-boxes and, in one rare instance, in the skull of a horse. In fact they will nest in just about any hole if the entrance is small enough. Perhaps trampers would be well advised to avoid lengthy yawns when passing through rifleman territory during the breeding season!

The breeding season, which starts around September, is put to good use. A pair of birds, which may remain together for life, is normally 'double brooded'. Both parents appear to be involved in the incubation and rearing of the first brood, but once these chicks have left the nest, the male bird will continue to feed them while his mate starts a second family. Curiously, the offspring from the first brood sometimes assist in feeding the second.

The felling of native bush and forest which followed the arrival of Europeans removed much of the riflemen's natural habitat. Yet today they are still common in most remaining primary forest and some secondary native bush. They are also occasionally seen in pine forests and other exotic forests where scatterings of native plants and trees are still present, and they may even be expanding their range.

1987, Watercolour, 23 × 33cm (9 × 13")

ASCENDING

Male South Island rifleman ascending decayed miro stick
J. Daysh collection

The Rockhopper Penguin

Eudyptes chrysocome

Rockhopper penguins are relatively small, noisy, very social birds which form large nesting colonies on many temperate sub-Antarctic islands. New Zealand islands such as Campbell Island, the Auckland Islands and the Antipodes Islands are all locations for very large rookeries, where the birds often nest together, shoulder to shoulder.

Like so many of the other penguins which congregate around the southern reaches of the New Zealand region, rockhoppers are delightfully amusing in appearance, particularly when they move about on land. Their near perfect adaptation to high-speed movement through water has definitely left the birds physically shortchanged when it comes to simple activities such as running and jumping. The sight of a rockhopper penguin hurriedly returning to the sea in its own unwieldy way is certainly something to raise a smile.

But although these penguins may appear comical creatures on land, the journeys they take in their marine habitats are no laughing matter. As they roam the cool southern seas in search of their foods (such as squid, fish and crabs), they face the ever-present danger of severe storms and a host of fierce hungry predators such as the sea leopard and sea lion.

During the breeding season, which begins around November, rockhoppers can be found in huge colonies of millions of birds. The nests they construct are loosely arranged from bits of grass and stones, pulled together around a slight indentation in the ground. The females will lay two eggs, but only one chick is successfully raised by both parents.

Rockhoppers are the most widely distributed of all penguins and the most abundant of the crested penguins, prolific enough for stragglers to be a reasonably familiar sight on the east coast beaches of mainland New Zealand.

The beautiful yellow tassels which form their crests just above the eyes were once sought after for decorative purposes. Understandably, the rockhoppers would not readily part with their 'hood ornaments' and in some parts of the penguins' wide-ranging domain, birds were slaughtered in great numbers. Today, though, with little need to fear people, rockhoppers are thriving and may even have the potential to expand their range still further.

1989, Pencil, 57 × 42cm (22 × 16½")

A DAY AT THE BEACH
A boy digging a pool for a straggler rockhopper penguin at Riversdale Beach, Wairarapa

THE ROCKHOPPER PENGUIN 93

The New Zealand Kingfisher

KOTARE
Halcyon santa vagans

Surrounded by a certain degree of myth and superstition, kingfishers, which are found throughout the world, are perhaps legendary birds. In my experience, to some people the mere mention of their name can give rise to feelings of fear or hate, whereas others may admire or even revere them. Yet, despite this reputation, the one and only New Zealand representative of the kingfisher family is a relatively secretive individual, living much of its life alone. It is most likely to be seen in the winter months, when it perches on telegraph wires and fence railings in open country in search of easier game.

When the bird is sitting on a fencepost by the roadside, the rich colouring of its back feathers seems boldly to advertise its presence like glowing blue neon. Yet, for its quarry, the kingfisher's tranquil pose and doleful gaze must render the bird almost invisible. The New Zealand kingfisher is by no means fussy about what it eats. Insects such as wetas, beetles and cicadas are taken, but the bird will also eat a variety of small animals such as worms, spiders, lizards, goldfish, crabs and mice and, on occasions, will kill and devour small birds such as silvereyes and fantails.

Nesting begins in September and the nest, effectively a tunnel, is excavated in a wide variety of places such as the clay banks of rivers and streams or farm tracks, as well as holes in trees, rotting tree stumps and even old chimneys.

The bird uses its long, powerful beak like a chisel to ensure that the tunnel is sufficiently long to accommodate up to three chicks. Kingfishers are very good parents, working hard to provide adequate food for their growing young. When the chicks have left the nest, adults have been known to fly rapidly at intruders, such as people and dogs, buzzing them several times simply for being in the vicinity.

As a strong defender of its family and a very adaptable bird, capable of feeding on a wide variety of food sources, the kingfisher has probably benefited from the changes brought by settlement and will more than likely continue to do so. Even after death, the body of the kingfisher is said to have the ability to calm violent winds and storms and to give beauty and prosperity. Reason enough, perhaps, not to underestimate this New Zealander!

1988, Watercolour, 30 × 38cm (11¾ × 15")

HALCYON DAYS

Juvenile New Zealand kingfisher watching German wasp
Bill and Jan Clinton-Baker collection

The Australasian Gannet

TAKAPU
Sula bassana serrator

Like so many birds of their order, Australasian gannets appear awkward when on land, but in the air they are magnificent fliers. Soaring over the sea, they suddenly plunge into a high-speed dive, pulling their wings back at the last moment before disappearing below the water, returning to the surface again at a different point. The purpose of these dives is, of course, to catch their food, which includes a variety of small fish and even tiny squid.

Despite the great spectacle of the gannets' feeding, the birds are probably best known for their breeding colonies where hundreds of very approachable birds roost and raise their young in close proximity to one another. Most breeding colonies are located on offshore islands; the only mainland colony is the famous one at Cape Kidnappers in Hawke's Bay.

The breeding season begins in September when adult birds establish bonds with one another through courtship displays. Nests are built using seaweed and grasses, arranged on the often guano-encrusted rock surfaces and cemented with droppings and gravel. Usually only one egg is laid. Both the egg and growing chick are raised and cared for by both parents. At the end of the breeding season all the gannets leave their colonies to roam the high seas and the waters of Australia and New Zealand.

Australasian gannets have substantially increased their population in New Zealand over the last 40 years and may even be expanding their range. With their breeding colonies protected as sanctuaries, these big-winged sea birds will continue to be seen gliding, almost effortlessly, over and around the shores of New Zealand.

1988, Pencil, 55 × 41cm (21¾ × 16¼")

PORTRAIT OF A GANNET AT CAPE KIDNAPPERS

The Little Shag

KAWAUPAKA
Phalacrocorax melanoleucos

Little shags are New Zealand's smallest and the most widespread cormorants, commonly seen on coastal and inland waters throughout the country. Their black and white plumage is extremely variable, with some individuals having only a white face and neck, whereas others have completely white undersides.

Diving and swimming for their prey, little shags eat crabs, shrimps, crayfish and marine fish around coastal waters as well as freshwater crayfish and fish, eels and insect larvae in inland waters.

The breeding season begins mainly about August, when birds may often gather together in rookeries to raise their young. Nests are built in among plants and trees and on rocky outcrops and are constructed of intermeshed twigs, sticks and plant materials to form a robust platform-like structure. Both the parent birds are involved in the nesting and may display aggressively to intruders.

The presence of increasing numbers of people near the little shags' watery habitat has not given them any great advantages, but these very sociable birds, while remaining wary, appear to live happily alongside humans around the wharves, jetties, rocky coastlines and inland rivers of New Zealand.

1989, Oil on panel, 60 × 45cm (23½ × 17¾")

THE LULL BEFORE A STORM
Two little shags resting on rocks at Riversdale Beach, Wairarapa

Bibliography

Barker, Lady Mary Anne, 1956. *Station Life in New Zealand*. (1st published 1870). 3rd edition, Whitcombe & Tombs, Auckland.

Cade, Tom J. and Digby, R. David, 1982. *The Falcons of the World*. William Collins Sons & Co., London.

Guthrie-Smith, H., 1910. *Birds of the Water, Wood and Waste*. Whitcombe & Tombs, Wellington.

Hammond, Nicholas and Everett, Michael, 1985. *Birds of Britain and Europe*. Pan Books, London.

Hanbury-Tenison, Robin, 1989. *Fragile Eden*. Century Hutchinson, Auckland.

Haufmann, John and Meng, Heinz, 1975. *Falcons Return*. William Morrow & Co., New York.

Hutton, F. W. (Ed.), 1905. *Nature in New Zealand*. 1st edition, Whitcombe & Tombs, Auckland.

Hutton, F. W. and Drummond, J., 1923. *The Animals of New Zealand*. 4th edition, Whitcombe & Tombs, Auckland.

Morris, Rod and Smith, Hal, 1988. *Wild South*. Century Hutchinson/TVNZ, Auckland.

Robertson, C.J.R. (Ed.), 1985. *Complete Book of New Zealand Birds*. Reader's Digest, NSW.

Smith, H. Easom, 1976. *Modern Poultry Development*. Spur Publications Co., USA.

Falla, Dr R.A. (et al.), 1948. *New Zealand Forest-Inhabiting Birds*. 2nd Edition, Forest and Bird Protection Society New Zealand Inc., Wellington.